Imagination Station
Exploring The Trailblazing Life of Pauli Murray

Written by
Avani and Sandesh Rao

Illustrated by
Deborah FitzGerald

Imagination Station
Exploring The Trailblazing Life of Pauli Murray

Written by Avani and Sandesh Rao

Illustrated by Deborah FitzGerald

Edited by Frank Monahan

PUBLISHED BY

Rocket Science Productions LLC

ISBN: 978-1-945355-90-5
Hardback ISBN: 978-0-9821823-2-1
e-ISBN: 978-0-9821823-3-8
Library of Congress Control Number: 2019930945

~ For Asha and her fellow friends,
children of a generation of limitless possibilities ~

Good morning girls and boys!
It's a lovely day for a field trip in the Imagination Station.

We will have the honor of meeting someone
very special and brave.

Come, shuffle in line—single formation!
There is so much to learn today from **Ms. Pauli Murray.**
Just this way, through the station!

Hello everyone, my name is Pauli Murray,
And I am here to tell a little bit about my story.

My sweet dreams when I was young,
May to some have seemed far-flung.

But with a little courage and self-esteem,
These nighttime thoughts became more than just a dream!

I was born in Baltimore, Maryland to very loving parents.
Auntie Pauline adopted me because of Mom and Dad's ailments.

In Durham, North Carolina, Auntie Pauline was a schoolteacher.
She taught me to dream big and think on my own —
not just be a people-pleaser.

Her life lessons would help me forever:

"Exceptional ability is nothing more than persistent endeavor."

To some people, being smart and hard working was just not enough.
Life in the 1920's for many groups of Americans was very rough.

Laws were in place that were just not right,
Leading to unfair treatment because we were not white.

These unfair rules promoted segregation,
And it was the law of the land for much of the nation.

Some colleges would not take me because of the color of my skin.
Being a girl in those times also limited what schools I could get in!

Auntie Pauline's advice made hard times conceivable to surmount.

Saying,
"Its not what you have, but what you are that counts."

Remembering Auntie's lessons, I started finding my own way,
I earned a spot in Hunter College in New York and had to move away.

Hard classes and multiple jobs made college not easy,
But with guidance from caring teachers, I got my degree.

From what I had experienced and what I had learned,
I became dedicated to represent people whose voices were unheard.

During The Great Depression, many lost or could not find work.
So, I helped people get jobs, build pride, and form a network.

I then spent time teaching kids
who could not read
Joining sounds to make
words, reading sentences, and
ultimately to succeed!

But my dreams to help others kept growing even bigger.
I had to learn the law to be a true civil rights crusader.

Being a minority woman, many law schools would deny me acceptance,
Rather than turning to anger, this motivated my drive and independence.

My motto was: "Don't get mad, get smart!"
I always asked WHY, and followed my heart.

So then I asked why, questioning those unfair rules
That prohibited me and others from going to a certain school.

Along the way, I met the wonderful First Lady Eleanor Roosevelt,
A strong woman who felt the same way
about discrimination as I felt.

Together we helped a Virginian sharecropper,
unfairly accused of a big crime.
Many of us hoped to reduce his sentence, but we ran out of time.

This opened my eyes to the injustices of segregation and racism,
Separation and hate were wrong—everyone should be welcome!

Why divide where someone could eat or sit because of how they look?
There is no reason for this, so this cause I undertook.

Separation in public based on color was simply unfair,
So we staged a restaurant sit-in, making sure it was a peaceful affair.

Of course many angry people tried to kick us out,
But some others listened to what we were upset about.

Rather than get mad, we got smart!
So, blacks and whites no longer ate apart.

We were able to help change the rule
By being activisits, yet still playing it cool.

It still surprises me just how big of a fuss
It was when I decided to sit in the front of the bus.

Eventually my journey led me to finally study the law,
When I was invited by Howard to be a lawyer after all the prior hoopla.

I was the only woman who was in my class,
But charging forward, all expectations I surpassed.

First Howard, then Berkley, and ending at Yale,
I studied the law extensively among mostly males.

I got a Doctorate in Law, the highest degree,
But, again there were no other Black students, except for me.

In positions of power, when I looked around,
I noticed hardly any women could be found!

So I gave speeches and helped pass laws to demand equal treatment.
Women deserve the same as men—we are equally brilliant!

In my elder years, it was last but not least,
That I became the first Black woman ordained as an Episcopal priest.

Questioning the limits should never be a bore,
When situations are unfair, be smart and cause an uproar.

With words and peaceful protest there is much to accomplish.
Think of all I was able to do, things that started as just a wish.

Pauli Murray lived with
determination and passion.

She took her wishes
and put them into action.

Do not worry about how you will be perceived.
It is more important to stand up
for what you believe.

So remember:

Have the biggest dreams.
These lead to more than it may seem.

About The Authors

Avani and Sandesh Rao are based out of Baltimore, MD where they live with their daughter Asha. They have always been inspired by people's acts of willpower that have brought change and success despite personal and societal circumstances. They hope their Imagination Station can introduce children to the big dreams and acts of courage of amazing people in history.

CPSIA information can be obtained
at www.ICGtesting.com
Printed in the USA
BVHW092005200222
629615BV00016B/373

9 781945 355905